THE
CROSS STITCH
TREASURY

THE
CROSS STITCH
TREASURY

SAMPLERS

GREENWICH EDITIONS

This edition published in 1995 by
Greenwich Editions
Unit 7
202-8 New North Road
London N1 7BJ

Produced by Marshall Cavendish Books, London

ISBN 0 862 880 653

British Library Cataloguing in Publication Data:
A catalogue record for this book is available from the British Library

Printed and bound in France by Partenaires

Some of this material has previously appeared in the Marshall Cavendish partwork
Discovering Needlecraft.

Contents

Foreword

Cross-stitch is probably the most popular embroidery technique practised in today's busy world, and it is certainly one of the oldest forms of textile decoration. It is a simple stitch that can be learned and enjoyed by young children and skilled stitchers alike to create amazingly intricate and interesting pieces which can become works of art or family heirlooms.

In fact, cross-stitch is a passion, practised by young and old, hobbyists and professionals, laid-back and perfectionist, and those lucky enough to be addicted will find much in this collection of projects to tempt them. The designs range from small-scale items such as greetings cards to intricate pieces that are highly realistic interpretations of familiar objects. So, if you love cross-stitch, pick up your needle, choose your chart and begin ...

Counted cross-stitch

Probably the oldest embroidery stitch of all, and certainly one of the quickest and easiest, counted cross-stitch is worked all over the world, in countries as far removed from each other as Mexico and India.

Cross-stitch has many uses. It can be worked as an outline or border, or as a filling stitch, and lends itself particularly well to lettering and motifs. Worked on canvas, it is very hardwearing and so makes a good choice for upholstery.

Counted cross-stitch is usually stitched on special evenweave fabrics, such as aida, hardanger, linda or binca, or on canvas, because this makes it easier to count threads and the whole effect of the stitch depends on its regularity. Each cross-stitch should make a perfect square, being worked down and across over an equal number of threads.

Designs for counted cross-stitch are always presented in chart form, where one cross or symbol or block of colour denotes a single stitch. Using one of these charts is easy — you literally count your way across the design.

There are several ways of working basic cross-stitch. Choose your method according to the fabric or canvas you will be working on. When working cross-stitch on canvas, or only making the odd cross-stitch here and there, it is best to complete each cross before moving on to the next one.

If you are working cross-stitch in rows on evenweave material, first work a line of diagonals in one direction, then cover them with 'top' diagonals, working in the opposite direction. By doing this you get a more even tension and finish. A variation of this, called

alternate cross-stitch involves working every other diagonal from right to left, then filling in the gaps by working another row of diagonals in the same direction, before working the top diagonals in the same way. This ensures an even more regular tension and so is a particularly good choice if you want to fill a very large area with cross-stitch.

One rule applies to all methods: the top diagonal stitches must always lie in the same direction. If they do not, they will reflect the light differently from the other stitches and will stand out clearly as mistakes. The only exception is when you actually want to produce an uneven or irregular effect.

OUTLINE STITCH

Use Holbein stitch, also known as double running stitch, in combination with cross-stitch to outline and emphasize solidly-stitched shapes and also to work decorative linear details. Like cross-stitch, Holbein stitch worked as an outline is most successful when sewn on an evenweave fabric so the fabric threads can be counted to ensure perfect regularity.

Holbein stitch looks exactly the same on both sides of the fabric. It can be worked in straight lines or stepped to make a zigzag line when outlining a diagonal row of cross-stitches. The finished result looks rather like a row of backstitch, at least on the front. All the stitches should be of identical length.

Cross-stitch motifs can be as varied and colourful as you wish. From floral designs and alphabets to geometric borders, plain or fancy, you can create some lovely effects. Don't stick to printed charts either — have a go at designing your very own motifs and borders. Take your inspirations from some of the stitched examples that appear here.

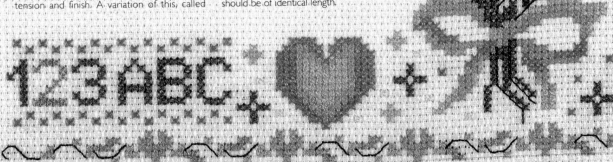

HOW TO WORK A SINGLE CROSS-STITCH

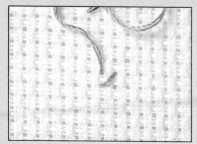

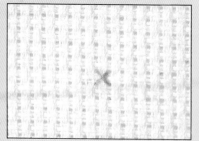

1 Make a diagonal stitch to the lower left, take the needle through to the back of the fabric and bring the needle back up at what will be the top left-hand corner of the cross.

2 Finish by taking the thread across the existing diagonal and inserting needle in bottom right-hand corner of cross. Count fabric threads to ensure each cross is worked over a square.

Various evenweave cottons and linens are specially produced with counted cross-stitch in mind. The most well-known is an evenweave cotton fabric called aida. Three of the samples below are made of the aida; the 22-count fabric is cotton hardanger. Each sample has a different 'count', which has been worked on the front in cross-stitch. The count refers to the number of holes in the fabric (those large enough to pass a needle and thread through) per inch. The holes are all exactly the same number of threads apart. As shown below, the count of your background fabric affects the size of each cross-stitch, and thus the scale and size of your finished design, quite considerably.

HOW TO WORK CROSS-STITCH IN ROWS

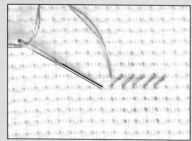

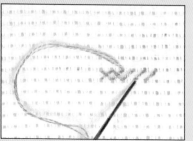

1 Make a diagonal stitch from top right to lower left. Bring needle out through the hole next to the start of the first stitch, ready to form the next, and continue.

2 At the end of the row change direction and complete the crosses by working another row of diagonals, this time from left to right, working each diagonal from upper left to lower right.

HOW TO WORK HOLBEIN STITCH AS AN OUTLINE

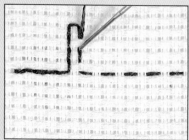

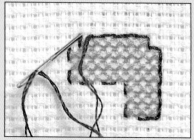

1 Work running stitches from right to left, following the outline of your shape. Each stitch should cover the same number of threads and the spaces in between should be the same size.

2 At the end of the row, turn work round and work back over the row just done, filling in the spaces with another row of running stitch. Keep the tension even at all times.

3 Outline a diagonal row of cross-stitch by alternately working horizontal and vertical running stitches. The Holbein stitch should outline the shape with a narrow, continuous line.

Baby's wall hanging

A commemorative picture with engaging embroidery designs will bring cross-stitch charm to the nursery.

YOU WILL NEED

- 10CM X 40CM WHITE 18-COUNT AIDA FABRIC
- MADEIRA 6-STRANDED EMBROIDERY COTTON, ONE SKEIN IN EACH OF THE FOLLOWING COLOURS: TAN 2011, YELLOW 0109, CREAM 0111, PALE PINK 0503, BLUE 1012, PEACH 0307, CORAL 0214, LIGHT GREY 1806,
- DARK GREY 1801, BLACK
- TAPESTRY NEEDLE
- 25CM NARROW RIBBON
- 8CM X 39CM STIFF CARD
- 10CM X 40CM WHITE BACKING FABRIC
- WHITE SEWING THREAD
- SHARPS NEEDLE

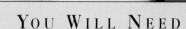

Baby's wall hanging

MAKING THE WALL HANGING

1 Place fabric pieces right sides together and pin. Sew round three sides in backstitch, eight squares in from the long edges and four squares in from the bottom edge, using sewing thread.

2 Remove all pins, trim corners and seams and turn right sides out. Gently push out bottom corners using scissor points and carefully insert cardboard stiffening through the top opening.

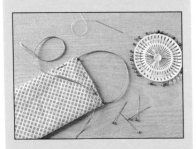

3 Fold top edges in. Insert ribbon ends through opening and pin to backing fabric, close to corners. Slip stitch opening, stitching through ribbon. Work two stitches of oversewing at corners to reinforce them.

This cross-stitch nursery wall hanging is a lovely way to greet a newborn baby. Nursery scenes in pretty colours are all part of creating an attractive environment for a baby and this wall hanging is child's play to stitch and make up.

STARTING TO STITCH

Work the design in cross-stitch using two strands of embroidery cotton throughout. Fold the aida fabric in half and then in half again to find the centre point. Following the chart on page 26, start at the centre of the design and work your way outwards. Work cross-stitch in rows wherever possible for a neater finish and make sure that all the top diagonals of your crosses lie in the same direction. Try not to dot your stitches all over the fabric – finish stitching each motif before you move on to the next one.

HOLBEIN STITCH

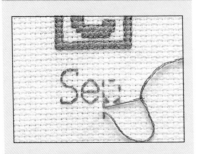

Holbein stitch is a straight stitch worked by stitching alternate lines of running stitch along the same line. First work a line of alternate running stitches across one intersection of the aida fabric so that the stitches and spaces are the same length as the crosses. Then work along the same line again in running stitches, filling in the spaces left between the first set of stitches.

Once you have embroidered all the motifs in cross-stitch, outline each one in Holbein stitch (see page 8 and below) using a single strand of grey thread. Choose the letters and numbers to make up the baby's name and birth date from the charts on page 26. Work the letters and numbers in Holbein stitch using one strand of grey thread.

FINISHING TOUCHES

When you have stitched the design, make up the wall hanging following the steps (far left).

The cardboard stiffening gives the wall hanging some body and weight, but if you prefer, you can eliminate it and simply fold back the

top edge of the aida fabric and stitch it to the backing fabric using slip stitch. Insert the ribbon as shown in the photograph and stitch it firmly in position.

Miniature sampler

This tiny sampler is perfect for a new stitcher to practise her skills or for an experienced needleworker to create a charming picture.

Miniature sampler

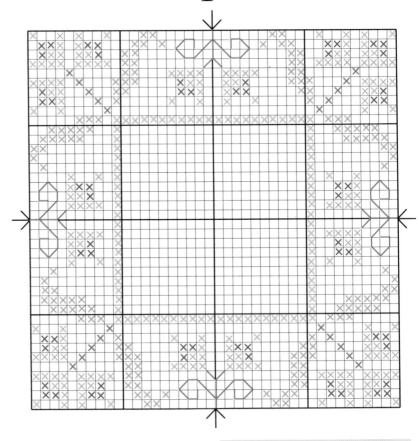

Samplers were originally worked by young girls, some only six or seven years old. Working such pieces provided a good opportunity for the girls to learn different embroidery stitches and to practise the alphabet. The young girls were considered inexperienced seamstresses by the older women who worked on fine garments and ornate tapestries and were frequently only allowed left-over cotton and yarn from other projects. For this reason many antique samplers are worked in a great variety of colours. More advanced samplers were often stitched to commemorate a birth or a new home, while some were used to learn and illustrate religious verses.

ORDER OF WORK

Follow the chart on the right, in which one coloured square represents one stitch. Use two strands of cotton in the needle throughout to work the design.

Fold the fabric in half and then in half again to find the centre and match it to the arrows on the chart. Count out from the centre and begin by stitching the square inner border, using gold (2213). Count carefully; if the square is not positioned correctly, you may find that you run out of fabric.

Next, stitch the leaves at each corner of the square using mid green (1703) and the stalks for the corner flowers in dark green (1705). The outer petals of the blooms are worked using dusty pink (0812) and the centres are plum (0810). To finish each flower, place a single cross-stitch on the end as indicated. The smaller flowers in the centre of each side are worked as for the corner flowers but stitching only two blooms instead of three. Their stalks are worked in backstitch, using two strands of dark green.

WORK OF ART

Once you have finished stitching the main part of the design, personalise the sampler by adding your initials and either the year you were born or the year you stitched it using backstitch and two strands of plum.

Mount and frame the picture following the instructions that are provided with the frame. As this design uses small amounts of cotton, you could use left-over threads to create alternative effects. Try bright primary colours to make a child's sampler, or combine orange, coral and turquoise for a more modern feel.

be creative

Make the sampler for a friend or relative to celebrate a birthday, christening or wedding anniversary. Choose an alphabet from one of the charts given on pages 26 to 32.

First home sampler

Celebrate the day you move into your first home as a couple by working this beautiful sampler in easy cross-stitch.

First home sampler

YOU WILL NEED

- 40CM X 50CM 14-COUNT WHITE AIDA FABRIC
- MADEIRA 6-STRANDED EMBROIDERY COTTON IN THE FOLLOWING COLOURS: 2 SKEINS EACH OF ROSE PINK 0505, BLUE GREEN 1109 AND EMERALD 1301; 1 SKEIN EACH OF PALE PEACH 2308, SALMON 0403, ORANGE 2307, OCHRE 2209, YELLOW 0109, PALE GREEN 1211, OLIVE 1408, CHARCOAL 1810 AND WHITE
- TAPESTRY NEEDLE
- READY-MADE FRAME AND MOUNT

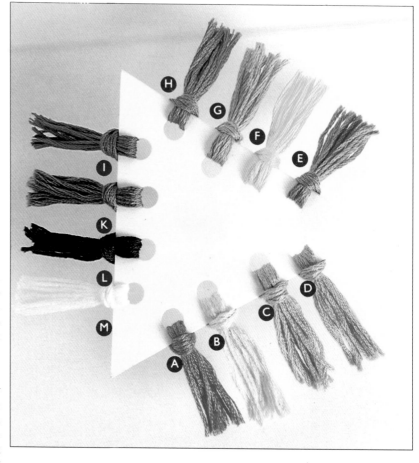

The sampler is worked in cross-stitch on 14-count aida fabric. By adding the names of the newly-weds and the date of the wedding, you can make this special sampler as a wedding gift to be treasured.

PREPARING TO STITCH

Each cross-stitch is worked over one square of the aida fabric. Find the centre of your fabric by folding the material in half, first lengthways and then widthways. Mark the centre of the fabric with horizontal and vertical tacking stitches that can easily be removed later. Now calculate the central point of the chart on pages 28 and 29, and mark it in pencil.

You would normally begin stitching at the centre to ensure that the finished sampler is positioned in the middle of the fabric, with opposite seams of identical widths. But in this case the centre is just below where you will be stitching the date. It is best to leave the letters and numbers until you have finished all the other stitching so that you can position them correctly within the context of the surrounding stitching.

The colours selected for the sampler (above) are a particularly attractive combination of pinks, browns and greens. Arrange samples on a card and label them for easy reference as you sew.

KEY

Madeira 6-stranded embroidery cotton, as used in the sampler:

A	0505	G	1211
B	2308	H	1109
C	0403	I	1301
D	2307	K	1408
E	2209	L	1810
F	0109	M	white

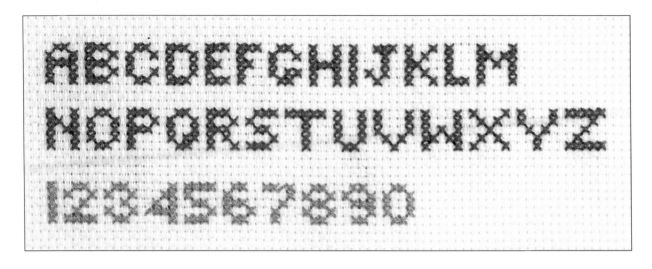

WORKING THE SAMPLER

Work with the sampler stretched taut on a hoop or a frame. As you stitch, follow the black and white symbols chart on pages 28 and 29. Each symbol represents a single cross-stitch, worked with two strands of cotton. Each colour used in the sampler is represented by a different symbol.

Begin with the roof of the house in two strands of ochre (2209), followed by the hedge and trees. Work the ribbon and bells, the bride and groom, the four-leaf clovers and the hearts. Then work the surrounding border. Stitch the two dogs, then work the motifs above the lettering. Work the bowl of fruit, then the border in two shades of green, followed by the two rose bushes, the hearts and the two borders above. Finally, outline the piece with a border of blue green, ochre, pale peach and white.

WORKING THE LETTERING

To work out the position of the lettering of the names and date, see the steps below. The lettering is worked in charcoal (1810) to a depth of five cross-stitches.

FINISHING THE SAMPLER

When completed, press the embroidery lightly on the wrong side. Then mount and frame the sampler following the steps on page 20.

HOW TO PLAN CROSS-STITCH LETTERING

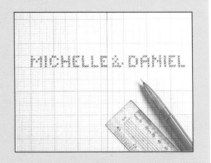

1 Use the sample alphabet above to spell out the names of the couple on graph paper, allowing one clear space between each of the letters and two clear spaces between the words.

2 Count the number of graph paper squares which the names and spaces have taken and divide it in half. Mark the exact halfway point of the lettering on the graph paper with a line.

3 Match the centre point of the lettering to the vertical centre line of the stitched sampler. Stitch from the centre outwards, following your graph paper plan. Repeat for the date below the names.

Rose sampler

Embroider a traditional cross-stitch sampler with vibrant red roses
for a personal and everlasting gift.

Rose sampler

Lovers of roses will appreciate this charming sampler which is worked throughout in counted cross-stitch. The colours used are fresh and lively and this gives the roses a velvety, realistic look. The central panel is worked in a classic cross-stitch design, using rows of numbers and alphabets edged with stylised bows and flowers. Embroidered samplers make lovely keepsakes and are a traditional way of marking special occasions such as births, weddings and new homes.

This rose sampler can be personalised by adding a name or a message using the charted alphabet letters on pages 26 to 32; the heart at the top edge can be left blank or filled in with intertwining initials. The simple frame echoes the natural theme of the sampler, which would look good in any setting.

GOOD WORKING ORDER

The basic rule of working any embroidery picture is to keep the design central by stitching from the middle outwards: this will also avoid distorting the fabric. Using two strands of cotton and following the chart opposite and key below, begin with the central alphabet panel. Embroider the red bow using crimson (0210) and scarlet (0513) and then work the border leading out from the bow using coral (0214) and leaf green (1305). Fill in the wavy line using carnation (0413) and stitch the alphabet in dove grey (1808). Next, work the alphabet and letters at the bottom using dove grey and soldier blue (1712), before decorating the alphabet at the top in the same colours. Complete the central panel by stitching the pink and red borders at the top and bottom and in between the rows of letters using carna-

tion (0413), scarlet (0513), crimson (0210) and fern (1502).

BORDER LINES

You are now ready to stitch the rose border. Work one complete area at a time, stopping where there is a natural break in the pattern. For instance, starting at the top left-hand corner, work the corner section consisting of two open roses and two buds, together with their foliage: stitch all the foliage first and then the roses themselves. The greenery is worked in leaf green (1305), apple green (1501), fern (1502) and moss (1314) and the roses in coral (0214), crimson (0210), scarlet (0513) and carnation (0413). Once you have a particular colour in your needle, work nearby parts of the design which are of the same colour. Next stitch the open rose with buds and foliage at the top and bottom. Continue until you have embroidered your way all around the border.

Finally, stitch the heart at the top in coral (0214) and scarlet (0513) and fill in the geometric outline border using moss (1314) and crimson (0210). Now that the embroidery is complete, you can frame the rose sampler as shown in the steps overleaf.

KEY

Madeira 6-stranded embroidery cotton, as used in the sampler:

A	1314	O	0214
C	1305	P	0413
E	0210	R	1502
L	1501	S	1712
N	0513	T	1808

bright idea

Frames and mounts are the finishing touch to a piece of needlework – so select them with care to complement the style of the work being framed. While a specialist framing shop will be able to frame the work for you, they also sell everything you need to do the job yourself. An expert in the shop will be able to advise you on the different styles and varieties of frame available, and will also be able to help you choose the colour and size for a mount and cut it for you if no standard size will fit your work. When you buy your frame, remember to get the correct tape and tacks, along with cord for hanging and screw-in hooks to attach it with. You are now ready to put the finishing touch to your work!

HOW TO FRAME THE SAMPLER

1 Press the sampler pulling it into shape, then assemble all the parts of your frame and mount, along with strong adhesive tape, thin tacks, a hammer and masking tape to complete the job.

2 Place the sampler face up on top of the lining card, measuring carefully around all the edges to ensure that the stitched area is absolutely centred on the card, so that it can be secured in place.

3 Secure the sampler in place on the lining card using tape adhesive. Take care to keep the sampler absolutely stiff and unpuckered, or it will not lie flat in the frame when finished.

4 With the frame face down, position the mount in the frame and then fit the sampler, mounted on the lining card, face down in the frame. Add the backing board on top of the lining card.

5 To keep the backing firmly in place, hammer tacks into the inside back of the frame so that they protrude by about 3mm. Take care not to damage the back with the hammer as you knock in the tacks.

6 To finish the back, use thick adhesive tape to mask the edges of the frame and the backing board. Attach a small screw-in hook on each side of the frame to fix cord for hanging (see box above).

Victorian sampler

Step back in time and create your own period sampler
with traditional motifs, borders and lettering.

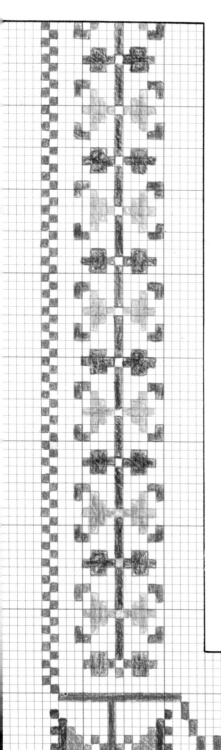

Victorian sampler

This magificent cross-stitch sampler is based on traditional Victorian motifs and borders, combined with two different styles of alphabet and a set of numerals. Stylized birds – doves, peacocks, bluebirds, a swan and a cockerel – are featured, each with its own distinctive characteristics. The trees include both conifers and tree-of-life designs, while the various borders are either simple and geometric or more floral. A flower basket and an ornate urn are also incorporated into the sampler along with tulip and carnation motifs and single geometric devices.

An alphabet of capital letters is stitched in blue, while another alphabet of lower-case letters is worked in a soft pink together with a set of numerals. As well as looking decorative, these letters may well be useful in other cross-stitch or needlepoint projects where you want to add initials, words or dates.

To enhance the Victorian feel of this sampler, lovely soft colours of Madeira 6-stranded cotton have been chosen for the embroidery – sage greens, rose pinks, old golds and mid blues. The evenweave fabric is a natural-coloured aida which gives the impression of an antique linen fabric. A simple dark wooden frame without a mount works best with this kind of sampler, as it does not detract from the detail in the embroidery and is also in keeping with the way traditional samplers were originally displayed.

BEFORE YOU BEGIN

Oversew or bind the edges of the aida fabric to prevent them from fraying as you stitch.

YOU WILL NEED

- 44CM X 50CM 14-COUNT NATURAL-COLOURED AIDA FABRIC
- MADEIRA 6-STRANDED EMBROIDERY COTTON IN THE FOLLOWING COLOURS: ONE SKEIN IN EACH OF MUSTARD 2203, DARK MUSTARD 2213, PINKY BROWN 2312, CRIMSON 0407, ROSE PINK 0812, DULL BLUE 1712, MID BLUE 1012, JADE 1203, PALE SAGE GREEN 1604; 2 SKEINS IN DARK SAGE GREEN 1602
- TAPESTRY NEEDLE
- SLATE FRAME

Fold the fabric in half each way and mark the centre horizontal and vertical lines with running stitches in a brightly-coloured sewing thread. This will help you when you are counting the stitches from the chart, and can be easily removed when the sampler is complete. Mark the centre lines on the chart in pencil to correspond. Stretch the fabric in a slate frame so that it is kept taut as you stitch. This will give

The border below runs along the lower edge of the sampler. It features stylized carnations worked in crimson, rose pink and dark sage green. The side border is stitched in mustard, dark mustard and pale sage green.

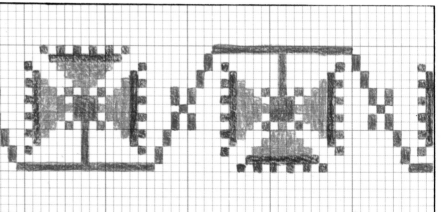

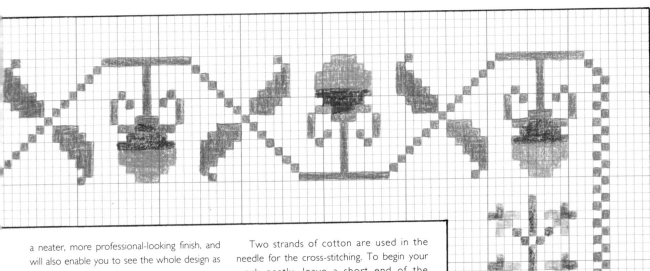

a neater, more professional-looking finish, and will also enable you to see the whole design as you progress.

The sampler is shown on the chart on pages 30 and 31. Each symbol on the chart equals one cross-stitch, which is worked over one square of the aida fabric; the key shows you which colours to use. Count the squares with symbols and the spaces in between them very carefully, as accuracy is important if all the borders are to join up correctly. The spacing between the letters and numerals is important, too, to give a balanced look to the alphabets.

STITCHING THE SAMPLER

It is a good idea to work the sampler from the centre outwards, as in this way you can be sure that it will be correctly positioned on the fabric. The crimson (0407) heart is a suitable motif to begin with; as it is slightly below the centre marked point on the chart, count out the number of aida squares from the centre down to the top of the heart and start stitching here.

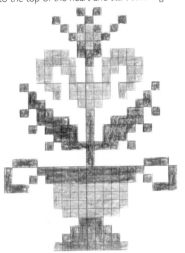

Two strands of cotton are used in the needle for the cross-stitching. To begin your work neatly, leave a short end of the embroidery cotton at the back of the fabric and make the first few stitches over it to secure it. To finish off, pass the needle under the last few stitches at the back of the work. Stitch one area of colour at a time, and do not take long lengths of thread across the back between areas. These will get caught up in subsequent stitching and may show through at the front when the sampler is mounted.

When the heart is complete, add the ribbons in rose pink (0812) and the doves in mid blue (1012) and pinky brown (2312). Counting outwards from the doves, work the cockerel on the left and the swan on the right. Complete the row with the bluebirds in mid blue. Next work the wavy line above the birds in pale sage green (1604), and work the lower-case alphabet and the numerals in rose pink. Count the spaces between the letters very carefully and add the small geometric motifs in dark mustard (2213) and dull blue (1712) when you come to them on the chart.

The twisted border between the two alphabets is worked in dark sage green (1602) and pale sage green, and the capital letters are mid blue. Add a geometric motif, a tulip and a flower basket at the end of the alphabet, as well as three tiny diamond shapes in pinky brown. To complete the top of the sampler, stitch the strawberry border in rose pink, crimson and dark sage green.

The upper border of the sampler shows a row of strawberry motifs. The border for the right-hand side is worked with a different pattern to the left-hand side, but is stitched in the same colours. The flower in the urn on the final row of the sampler is worked in crimson and rose pink.

You can now continue with the lower half of the sampler. The border below the row of birds is worked in dark sage green. Then comes a row of trees in different colours and patterns. The central tree is worked entirely in dark sage green, while the ones on either side are stitched in two colours. Smaller trees worked in pinky brown are placed between the five large ones. When the trees are complete, work a wavy geometric line of stitching, this time in the pale sage green, below them.

The final row of motifs in the sampler shows a flower urn in the centre and two splendid peacocks on either side. Work the peacocks in mid blue with dull blue for the tail and crest. The tail decorations are jade (1203) and dark mustard, the eyes are jade and the legs dark mustard. Two identical flowers in mustard (2203), dark sage green and jade come at the ends of this row. The lower border consists of carnation flowers in rose pink and crimson with dark sage green stems. To finish off the sampler, stitch the side borders. The inner borders are two different floral designs in shades of mustard and pale sage green, and the outer border is simply made up of alternating crosses worked in the dark sage green.

MAKING UP THE SAMPLER

Before you remove the sampler from the slate frame, check that you have not missed any of the cross-stitches, as these will be difficult to add once the fabric is mounted over card and the design is framed. Finish off all your thread ends neatly, weaving them into a few stitches

be creative

As well as showing skill in stitching, a sampler was also useful as a pattern library of motifs which could be used in other pieces of work.

In the same way, you could stitch any of the motifs on this sampler onto a small piece of evenweave or aida fabric to use as a greetings card, a bookmark or a pot pourri sachet. Use up the stranded cotton left over from this project, or odds and ends from your work basket.

The bookmark shown here was made by taking one carnation motif and a section of the right-hand border and working them onto a piece of white aida fabric. To balance the design you will need to add the alternating cross-stitches to the left-hand side of the border.

at the back of the work and cutting them off short so that they do not show through at the front and spoil the finished effect.

Take the fabric off the frame and press from the wrong side over a lightly padded surface so as not to flatten the stitches. Stretch the sampler over a piece of acid-free

mounting board and either tape the edges or use string to lace the edges and frame as you wish.

Conifer trees as well as tree-of-life motifs are worked in shades of sage green, mustard, pinky brown and jade in the band below.

Ribbon sampler

A swirling ribbon design finishes off this simple cross-stitch sampler to perfection. Add the name of your choice to complete it.

The ribbon sampler chart is shown on page 32. Each symbol on the chart represents one cross-stitch. The key shows you which colours of stranded cotton to use in the needle. A charted alphabet is also shown from which you can select the letters you need for the name you wish to stitch.

BEFORE YOU BEGIN

Mark the centre of the fabric horizontally and vertically with tacking stitches to help you to position the stitches correctly. Before stitching your name, chart the letters on a piece of graph paper to make sure they fit comfortably within the inner border (see page 16).

STARTING TO STITCH

Find the centre point of the name and count out from here to establish where to begin stitching the first letter. Alternatively, begin stitching at the centre letter and work outwards from here, using pink for the name. Work with two strands of cotton in the needle throughout.

Next work the inner border around the name in blue and yellow. Finally stitch the ribbons and bows in pale, mid and dark green.

FINISHING THE PIECE

When the sampler is complete, press lightly from the back over a padded surface to keep the texture of the stitchwork. Mount and frame the sampler as you wish (see page 20).

YOU WILL NEED

- 30CM X 25CM 27-COUNT CREAM EVENWEAVE LINEN
- MADEIRA 6-STRANDED EMBROIDERY COTTON, ONE SKEIN IN EACH OF THE FOLLOWING COLOURS: PALE GREEN 1604, MID GREEN 1401, DARK GREEN 1403, PINK 0807, BLUE 1004, YELLOW 2203
- TAPESTRY NEEDLE
- GRAPH PAPER

Baby's wall hanging

Use this chart and key (right and opposite) to work the cross-stitch design for the wall hanging. Each square on the chart represents one cross-stitch worked over one square of aida fabric. Take care when matching each section of the design either side of the 'overlap' line. Make up your own messages using the letters and numbers on the chart opposite.

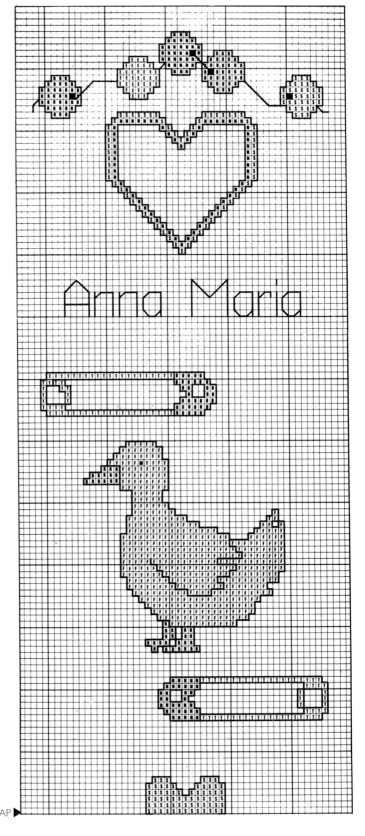

KEY		
A Tan 2011		**O** Blue 0102
E Yellow 0109		**R** Peach 0307
F Cream 0111		**S** Coral 0214
M Black		**T** Lt grey 1806
N Pink 0503		■ Grey 1801

OVERLAP ▶

KEY

A	Tan 2011	O	Blue 0102
E	Yellow 0109	R	Peach 0307
F	Cream 0111	S	Coral 0214
M	Black	T	Lt grey 1806
N	Pink 0503	■	Grey 1801

25 September

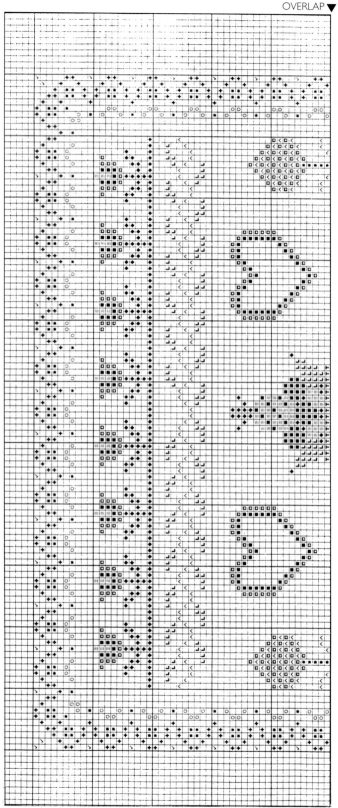

First home sampler

Use this chart and key (below and facing page) to work the cross-stitch design for the First home sampler. Each square on the chart represents one cross-stitch worked over one square of aida fabric. Take care when matching each section of the design either side of the 'overlap' line.

KEY

Madeira cotton, as used in the First home sampler:

charcoal 1810	pale green 1211
white	pale peach 2308
emerald 1301	blue 1109
orange 2307	yellow 0109
rose pink 0505	ochre 2209
olive 1408	salmon 0403

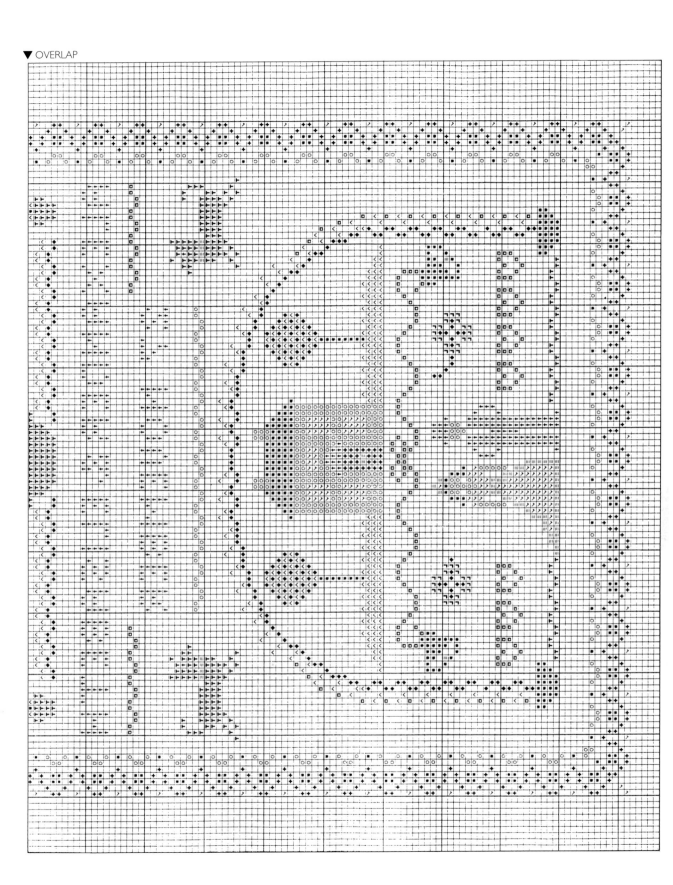

Victorian sampler

Use this chart (right and facing page) and the key (below) to work the cross-stitch design for the Victorian sampler on page 21. Each square on the chart represents one cross-stitch worked over one square of aida fabric. Take care when matching each section of the design either side of the 'overlap' line.

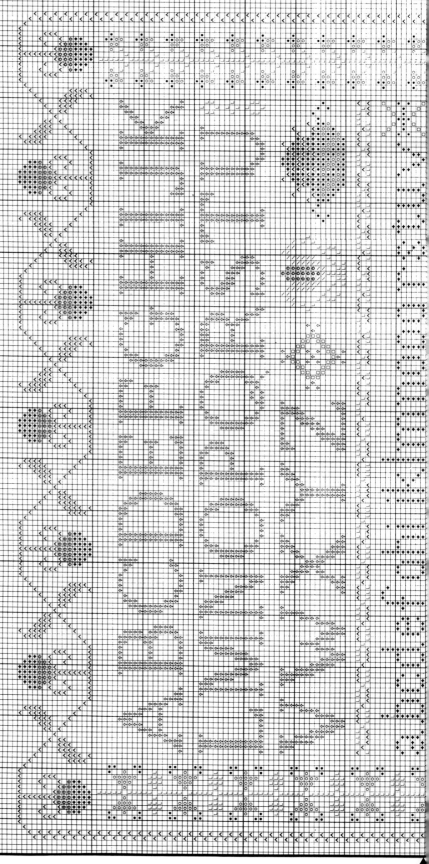

KEY

Madeira 6-stranded cotton, as used in the Victorian sampler:

- ● Dark mustard (2213)
- ✳ Crimson (0407)
- ⬆ Mid blue (1012)
- ☐ Dull blue (1712)
- ∧ Dark sage green (1602)
- ⊥ Jade (1203)
- ∟ Pale sage green (1604)
- ◺ Pinky brown (2312)
- ⊚ Mustard (2203)
- ✚ Rose pink (0812)

ERLAP

Ribbon sampler

Use this chart and key to work the cross-stitch design for the Ribbon sampler. Each square on the chart represents one cross-stitch worked over one square of aida. Add the name of your choice, in pink cotton (0807), using either Holbein stitch or cross-stitch.

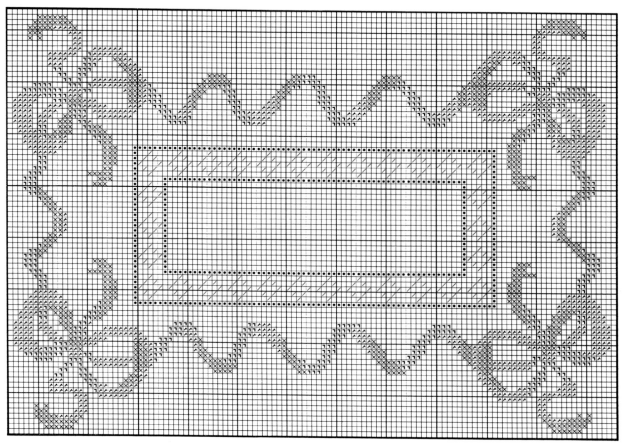

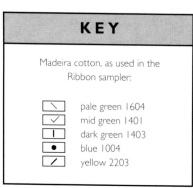

KEY

Madeira cotton, as used in the Ribbon sampler:

⟍	pale green 1604
✓	mid green 1401
I	dark green 1403
●	blue 1004
∕	yellow 2203